Songs of the Sailor

Working Chanteys at Mystic Seaport

Compiled and edited by Glenn Grasso
Transcribed by Marc Bernier

Mystic Seaport Museum, Inc., Mystic, Connecticut

Dedication

This work is dedicated to Joanna Colcord, Richard Henry Dana, William Doerflinger, Frederick Pease Harlow, Stan Hugill, John and Alan Lomax, Cecil J. Sharp, Frank Shay, Cicely Fox Smith, W. B. Whall, and all of the other individuals who preserved this music and tradition. Their foresight has given future generations much to play, sing, and record. Without their efforts, sea music would have surely been lost to history.

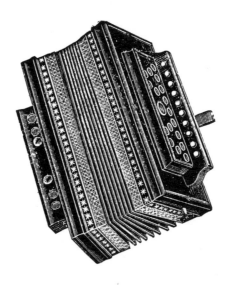

Contents

Mystic Seaport
75 Greenmanville Avenue
Mystic, CT 06355

Grasso, Glenn.
    Songs of the sailor: working chanteys at Mystic Seaport / compiled and
edited by Glenn Grasso; transcribed by Marc Bernier. — [1st ed.] — Mystic,
Conn.: Mystic Seaport Museum, [c1998]
    p.: ill., music; cm.
    Bibliography: p.
    Includes glossary.

    1. Sea songs. 2. Historical museums - Interpretive programs. I. Mystic
Seaport Museum.

M1977.S2G7
ISBN 0-913372-84-6

First Edition

Illustration credits: Page 6 – Charles Rosner, MSM 71.301.8; Page 10 – Gordon Grant, reprinted from
Joanna Colcord's *Songs of American Sailormen* with the permission of W. W. Norton & Co.; Page 21 –
Gordon Grant, MSM 59.790; Page 24 – Gordon Grant, reprinted from Joanna Colcord's *Songs of
American Sailormen* with the permission of W. W. Norton & Co.; Page 36 – Gordon Grant, reprinted
from Joanna Colcord's *Songs of American Sailormen* with the permission of W. W. Norton & Co.;
Page 44 – Charles Rosner, MSM 71.301.5; Page 49 – Gordon Grant, reprinted from Joanna Colcord's
Songs of American Sailormen with the permission of W. W. Norton & Co.; Page 56 – engraving from
Harper's Weekly, November 11, 1882, MSM 83.110.2; Page 62 – Gordon Grant, MSM 59.749.

Cover: "At the Wheel" by Frank Brangwyn, an engraving that appeared in *Scribner's Magazine* for July
1893, Claire White-Peterson photo, MSM 94-1-44.

Preface

This work was originally conceived as a companion piece to "Songs of the Sailor," a CD released by the Mystic Seaport chanteymen in 1997. Included are the words and music to all of the songs on the CD, interpretations and explanations for each of the songs, and some variants. This work is not meant to be the final word on the subject; Stan Hugill's *Shanties from the Seven Seas* has already fulfilled that role. Rather, this is designed to be an overview of chanteying at Mystic Seaport, the Museum of America and the Sea. Mystic Seaport is one of the only places in the world where chanteys are used to perform shipboard work. All year long, there is a music show on the grounds of Mystic Seaport. During the spring, summer, and fall, our demonstration squad shows our visitors what it was like to set sails on a nineteenth-century square-rigger. They have the advantage of doing the job in good weather, tied to the dock, but the work is still heavy, requiring a group effort. They set, raise, and furl sails, raise anchors, march around a capstan, and row and raise a whaleboat. The chantey staff works with the demonstration squad to coordinate the efforts of the group. Sometimes this requires minor alterations, as the demonstration squad is working at a museum, not on board a working vessel out at sea.

Perhaps the greatest alteration is some of the terminology. Chanteys were sung by men far from shore. Performing at a family museum requires some modification of the salty language used by deepwater sailors. Also, many derogatory racial terms have been removed by staff musicians. What was once common in both print and speech is no longer acceptable. The times have changed. As is the case with any art form based on an oral tradition, several variants of the same songs exist. This is true even within our ranks. There are currently eight musicians at Mystic Seaport, and we each have our own ideas about how things should be done. This diversity within the music program is our greatest strength.

CHARLES RUSNER '??

Introduction

Going To Sea

Human beings have always been filled with a great curiosity. There has always been a desire to discover new things by exploring the unknown. Perhaps the greatest unknown is the sea. Standing upon the shore and looking out over a vast expanse of water, one cannot help but wonder what lies just beyond the horizon. This sense of wonder led the human race to build ships. Small at first, these vessels allowed people to go to another world, the world of the sea.

Sailing ships would explore nearby waters, with each voyage going farther than the last. Occasionally, a few brave captains and sailors took their vessels far from land in search of new places. The daring of Leif Eriksson, Christopher Columbus, Ferdinand Magellan, and others opened up more of the world than anyone had ever imagined. This had both positive and negative results. By the 1600s, European explorers had begun colonizing the places that they had discovered. In the 1700s, trade between the colonies and the mother countries was booming. Sailing ships carried the products of the world over the oceans. War and aggression brought military power to the sea. In the far corners of the world, there were few people whose lives did not, in some way, have a connection to the sea.

There was no artificial power to move vessels over the water. No gasoline, diesel fuel, or nuclear power existed, only human power, animal power, and the power of the wind. One or two people could row a small boat or dozens could row a Roman warship or a Viking ship. The wind, however, made things much easier. Stretching canvas out before the wind saved the strength of the crew. It could move a boat faster, longer, and for a greater distance than the human power on board. Plus, the wind was free to any who would harness it.

This is not to say that there was no hard work involved with sailing a ship. Despite the fact that the wind actually pushed the boat along, there was much work to be done to catch the wind. Sails had to be raised up and adjusted before the wind. When the wind began blowing too hard, those same sails had to be put away before they ripped or knocked the vessel over on its side. Before a ship even left port, the anchor needed to be raised. If the vessel stopped anywhere, the same anchor had to be raised time and time again. All of this work was done by the crew on board. They had the basic mechanical advantages of block-and-tackle and winch, but the crew was the power that moved things along.

What is a Chantey?

Although the English prefer to spell the word "shanty," the term "chantey" is most likely derived from the French "chanter." *Cassell's French Dictionary* defines the word as follows: "v.i. To sing; to speak, read, etc., in a sing-song tone; to chirp, to carol, to warble, to crow." Indeed, the French word "chantez" is the command to "Sing!" The first chanteys were simply a few words yelled out, with the work being done on the emphasized syllable or word. As working a ship became more complicated, the songs used at work grew as well. Most of these work songs involved a lead singer and then a chorus response from the crew. Songs for hauling on ropes were different from songs used to march around a capstan, but in almost every case, one person sang the lead and the rest responded in the chorus.

The idea of coordinating the efforts of people with call-and-response songs seems to exist in almost every culture. For example, in China, there is a gorge where the equivalent of white-water rafting attracts tourists. They are flown in by helicopter for a two-hour trek down the rapids. The local Chinese then spend the next two days hauling the boats back up the river against the current. The leader cries out a one-line verse, then the people pulling on the rope attached to the boat respond with a chorus. The boat moves about three feet. Then they do it again. And again. They accomplish this with the same call-and-response type of chant that was found on nineteenth-century sailing ships, on railroad track-lining gangs, and in lumber camps. Almost any time that there was monotonous, labor-intensive, repetitious work, music was used to help people work together. In the days before auxiliary power, working to song was universal.

When a group of people gathered to do a job, they needed to work together as a unit. By working with one another, the group could accomplish tasks that would have been impossible to do individually. Such is the nature of teamwork. Chanteying on board sailing ships had many purposes. It coordinated the efforts of the crew by focusing their attention on the job and at the same time it took their minds off the difficulty of the heavy tasks at hand. It inspired teamwork among the crew by bringing them together to accomplish a common goal. Chanteying also set the crew apart from the officers on the ship. It demonstrated who was doing the work and who was giving the orders. It gave the crew a way to express their true feelings about the ship's officers without the risk of punishment. As a mental diversion while doing heavy physical work, as a tool to organize a group, and as an outlet for the crew to comment on shipboard life, chanteys played an important role in the sailors' lives. A good chantey, it was said, was worth "ten men on a line."

Why Did Chanteying Arise?

As ship design progressed in the mid-nineteenth century, the art of chanteying entered a "golden age." Sailing vessels were becoming bigger as the Industrial Revolution increased the demands made on shipping. Raw materials needed to be delivered to factories, and manufactured goods had to find their way to market. As vessels became larger and larger, their crews, proportionate to their size, were getting smaller. The ships were becoming longer, but also narrower. This sleek design increased their speed, but it also decreased the cargo-carrying capacity. This meant narrower profits for the owners. The ship owners, of course, wanted to increase their profits. They did what all corporations do when faced with tough economic times—they downsized. This meant fewer men to pay, but it also left fewer men on board to crew these vessels.

Two more factors contributed to the increase in the size and speed of sailing vessels. China was opened to American trade by treaty in 1844. The China tea trade demanded fast vessels because the tea would spoil if it remained on board too long. A quick passage meant better (and more expensive!) tea at the end of the voyage. Then gold was discovered at Sutter's Mill, California, in 1848. When word of the discovery reached the East, the California Gold Rush of 1849 began. San Francisco, which had once been a tiny mission town, turned into a small city almost overnight. More and more people wanted to go West to find their fortunes, but the real fortune was to be made by supplying the fledgling settlement. Anyone who could transport cotton canvas, picks, shovels, food, and manufactured goods to the miners could earn enormous profits. Speed became all-important. With less room for cargo, profit became linked directly with the ability to make quick passages. Chanteying on board American ships was about to explode.

Who Sang Chanteys?

Being a "chanteyman" was not an official position on board ship. The more experience that a sailor had, the higher his rank and pay. So it was with the ability to sing chanteys. It was something that a sailor would learn throughout the course of his sailing career. Some sailors had natural ability while some did not. Some liked to sing more than others, and some were appreciated more than others by the crew. Songs were passed from person to person. Few were ever written down. This oral tradition often resulted in many variants of the same song. Indeed, finding several variations of the same song is a good indicator that the song is authentically traditional. The oral tradition, however, had its advantages and disadvantages. On the one hand, it allowed people with no formal musical education to learn music and folklore. It also served to keep the music alive by constantly introducing new blood to the old songs. Unfortunately, the oral tradition resulted in countless variants being lost to history.

What Are the Roots of Chanteys?

The roots of sea music are the Anglo-Irish tradition and the African-Caribbean tradition. Each tradition has unique characteristics. African-Caribbean music tends to tell a story or present a poetic image within each verse. Harmony is often sung when multiple singers are present. It is rhythmically oriented, often syncopated, and open to improvisation. These characteristics hold true for much of the music produced by peoples of African cultural backgrounds, whether blues, gospel, jazz, or even rap. The rhythmic foundations of this style make it especially appropriate to shipboard work. On board ship, improvisation was important because a singer had to keep the song going until the work was finished.

Songs originating in the Anglo-Irish tradition tend to be sung in unison. While not a hard and fast rule, Anglo-Irish songs often tell a single story throughout. Each verse needs to appear in its proper place for the story to make sense. On board ship this sometimes meant that a story was cut short if the job was finished quickly. The song, like a tool, stopped when the work was done. At other times, the job took longer to complete. Then, the singer had to improvise, but the improvisation occurred at the end of the song.

As these two traditions came into contact with one another, characteristics of each crossed cultural lines. African terms became mixed in with Irish melodies. Irish songs took on African choruses. This resulted in work songs that told stories, used harmonies, and had driving rhythms. In America, these two distinct musical traditions melded to form a uniquely "American" style of chanteying.

Capstan Chanteys

Raising the anchor on a large sailing ship was the first heavy job for the crew. The job was long and difficult because of the way that the anchor was set. It required putting out chain or cable equal to seven times the depth of the water. As a result, most of the job of raising an anchor involved pulling the ship *up to* the anchor. Only then was the anchor raised off the bottom.

A capstan is a mushroom-shaped object with a row of holes along the top. Wooden bars are inserted into these "pigeonholes." Viewed from above with the bars in place, the capstan looks like the spokes of a wagon wheel without the outer rim. Lines or chain are wrapped around the body of the capstan, usually three times. Then, sailors march around the capstan pushing on the bars. To prevent the lines or chain from wrapping around and around into one big mess, one sailor "tails": he takes up the slack that comes in as the capstan turns. This insures that there are always three wraps, but not more, around the capstan. As the chain comes in, it is stored below in a chain locker.

Since working at the capstan meant marching around it, the music used at this job had a steady rhythm. The songs had verses and choruses and were designed to keep the sailors marching together. These jobs often took a long time, so capstan chanteys often told stories. Many times, the jobs turned out to be longer than the songs. If this happened, a good chanteyman had to improvise and make up verses to complete the job.

Capstan work at Mystic Seaport is performed on board the ship *Joseph Conrad*. The *Joseph Conrad*'s capstan is located on the fo'c's'le deck at the bow of the ship. Our demonstration uses one of the ship's 2,000-pound lifeboats to simulate the weight of the anchor. We use the capstan to raise the boat. The demonstration lasts about ten minutes. Raising anchor, a sailor might have to march around the capstan for hours.

Ebenezer
Capstan/windlass/pumps

I shipped on board of the Eb- en- ez- er
Ev- ry day 'twas scrub and grease her Ho- ly stone her and
scrape her down And if we growled they'd blow us down
Get a- long boys get a- long do Han- dy me boys so han- dy oh
Get a- long boys get a- long do Han- dy me boys so han- dy

12

I shipped on board of the *Ebenezer*
Every day 'twas scrub and grease her
Holystone her and scrape her down
And if we growled they'd blow us down

Chorus
Get along boys, get along, do
Handy me boys, so handy, oh
Get along boys, get along, do
Handy me boys, so handy

The old man was a drunken geezer
He could not sail the *Ebenezer*
Learned his trade on a Chinese junk
Spent 'most time down in his bunk

The first mate's name was Dickie Green, sir
The cruelest brute that you've ever seen, sir
Walking the deck with a bucko roll
May the sharks have his body and the devil have his soul

A Boston buck was second greaser
He used to ship in limejuice ships, sir
The Limey packets they got too hot
He cursed them all and he jumped the lot

We sailed away before a breezer
Bound away for Valparaiso
Round Cape Horn we lost her sticks
The mollyhawks picked up the bits

The *Ebenezer* was so old
She knew Columbus as a boy
It was pump her, bullies, night and day
To help her get across Liverpool Bay

Sailors could complain in song. Often they could sing about things that they would never be allowed to say outright. To avoid being punished, the chantey singer would have to disguise the names of the ship or the people about whom he was singing. When challenged, the singer could then claim that he was singing about different officers on a different ship. Since work was being done, the mates would often allow the crew this freedom to poke fun at them. It was one of the few times that a sailor could ever say anything negative out loud. This version is based primarily on the version found in Stan Hugill's *Shanties from the Seven Seas*.

Johnny Come Down To Hilo
Capstan

I've ne- ver seen the like since I've been born An

Ar- kan- sas farm- er with his sea boots on

John- ny come down to Hi- lo a poor old man So

wake her [and] shake her Oh wake that girl with the blue dress on

John- ny come down to Hi- lo a poor old man

I've never seen the like since I've been born
An Arkansas farmer with his sea boots on

Chorus
Johnny come down to Hilo, a poor old man
So, wake her, [and] shake her
Oh, wake that gal with the blue dress on
Johnny come down to Hilo, a poor old man

I love a gal across the sea
She's a 'Badian beauty and she says to me

Oh, Ginny's in the garden picking peas
The hair on her head grows down to her knees

Now, my wife died in Tennessee
They sent her jawbone back to me

I set that jawbone on the fence
And I ain't heard nothing but the jawbone since

So, hand me down my riding cane
I'm off to see my sweetheart, Jane

The ports of the southern United States are considered by Stan Hugill to have been a "shanty mart" of sorts. Sailors from many different places were working together on the waterfronts of Mobile, Alabama, New Orleans, Louisiana, and Savannah, Georgia. As men worked side by side, chanteys filled the air. Before long, themes and lyrics from the vast oral tradition developing among African Americans were being sung to old Irish melodies. In this chantey, lyric and melodic elements that later influenced the development of the blues are found.

This version of "Johnny Come Down to Hilo" was assembled at Mystic Seaport. It is a composite of several printed versions. All the roots of this version, whether printed or oral, were available to the nineteenth-century Southern singer. In addition to combining several sources, this version has eliminated some terms and phrases that are no longer acceptable. Just as our version is a blend, this capstan chantey is a fine example of the cultural blend to be found aboard a nineteenth-century sailing ship.

Liverpool Judies
Capstan

From Liv- er- pool to 'Fris- co a ro- vin' I

went To stay in that coun- try was my good in-

tent But drink- in' strong liq- uor like oth- er damn

fools Soon got me trans- port- ed back to Liv- er-

pool Sing- in' row_____ row bul- lies row Them

Liv- er- pool Ju- dies have got us in tow

From Liverpool to 'Frisco a-rovin' I went
To stay in that country was my good intent
But drinkin' strong liquor like other damn fools
Soon got me transported back to Liverpool

Chorus
Singin' row, row, bullies, row
Them Liverpool Judies have got us in tow

There's a smart Yankee packet lyin' out in the bay
Awaitin' a fair wind to get underway
But all of her sailors so sick and so sore
They drunk all their whiskey and can't get no more

Oh here comes the mate in a hell of a stew
He's lookin' for graft for us sailors ta [to] do
"Jib tops'l halyards!" he loudly does roar
It's lay along Paddy, you son of the shore

One night off Cape Horn I shall never forget
It's oft times I sigh when I thinks of it yet
We was roundin' Cape Horn with our main-skys'l set
We was roundin' Cape Horn with us all wringin' wet

And now we're a-haulin' way on to the line
When I thinks of it yet sure we had a good time
Them sea-boys box-haulin' their yards all around
To beat that flash packet called the *Thatcher MacGowan*

And now we've arrived in Bramleymoor Dock
Where them flash little judies to the pierhead flock
The barrel run dry and our five quid advanced
And I guess it's high time to get up and dance

Here's a health to the captain where e'er he may be
A friend to the sailor on land or on sea
But as for the chief mate, that dirty old brute
We hope when he dies a-ta [oh, to] Hell he'll skyhoot

Liverpool, England, was a major port for both merchant shipping and immigration in the nineteenth century. All of this activity made for a bustling waterfront, one with lots of distractions. Having a sailor "in tow" suggests being led around. The "Liverpool Judies" would gather along the docks, eagerly awaiting the sailors and their money to come on shore. Once ashore, the "Judies" could take advantage of both. A more benevolent reading might interpret "in tow" to be an imaginary ropeline that was tugging or trying to pull the sailor back to land or home where friends, lovers, and family reside. On land Jack Tar, the generic name for a sailor, was awkward, uneasy, and out of his element, but even out to sea he still could not escape the homesick thoughts that pulled him back to his native land. This chantey is sung in live performances around Connecticut by Cliff Haslam. Many people have learned it from him. The words are from Stan Hugill's *Shanties from the Seven Seas*.

Paddy Lay Back
Capstan

It was a cold and win- try mor- ning one De-
cem- ber (De- cem- ber) And all of me
mon- ey it was spent (spent spent) Oh where to it
went I can't re- mem- ber (re- mem- ber) So down to the
ship- ping of- fice I went (went went) Pad- dy lay
back (Pad- dy lay back) Take up your slack (take up your
slack) Take a turn a- round the cap- stan heave a
pawl (heave a pawl) A- bout ships sta- tions boys be han- dy (we're
han- dy) We're bound for Val- pa- rais- o round the horn

It was a cold and wintry morning one December (*Repeat:* December)
And all of me money it was spent (*Repeat:* spent spent)
Oh, where to it went I can't remember (*Repeat:* remember)
So down to the shipping office I went (*Repeat:* went went)

Chorus
Paddy lay back (Paddy lay back)
Take up your slack (take up your slack)
Take a turn around the capstan, heave a pawl (heave a pawl)
About ships to stations, boys, be handy (we're handy)
We're bound for Valparaiso, 'round the Horn

Now on that day there was a great demand for sailors (for sailors)
Oh, shipping for the colonies and for France (France France)
So I signed aboard a Limey bark the *Hotspur* (*Hotspur*)
And got paralytically drunk on my advance (my advance)

Now it was on the quarterdeck when I first saw 'em (saw 'em)
Such an ugly lot I never did see before (see before)
There was a bum and a stiff from every quarter (quarter)
And it made me poor old heart feel sick and sore (sick and sore)

Now there was Spaniards and Russians and Dutchmen (Dutchmen)
And Johnny Crapoes just across from France (France France)
Not a man amongst 'em spoke a word of English (English)
But they answered to the name of "month's advance" (month's advance)

Now some of our fellas had been drinking (drinking)
And I meself was heavily on the booze (booze booze)
So I sat upon me old sea chest a-thinkin' (a-thinkin')
That I'd go into me bunk and have a snooze (have a snooze)

Well, I woke up in the morning sick and sore-o (sore-o)
And I knew that I was outward bound again (bound again)
Then I heard a voice a-bawlin' at the door-o (door-o)
"Lay aft, men, and answer to your names" (to your names)

So I asked the mate a-which a-watch was mine-o (mine-o)
He said you'll soon find out a-which is which (which is which)
Then he beat me down and kicked me hard a stern-o (stern-o)
And he called me a dirty, lousy son of a fish (son of a fish)

Well, they called us up on deck to reef the topsails (topsails)
Belaying pins were flyin' around the deck (around the deck)
And the cook was stealin' brandy from the captain (captain)
Lord, I know we'll never make it on this wreck (on this wreck)

This chantey is of Irish origin. The song talks about our hero, "Paddy," and the circumstances of his arrival on board. Once on board, he finds his co-workers to be "an ugly lot," the officers abusive, and the ship unsafe. Not surprisingly, many versions of this song have him quickly leaving the ship before anything else can go wrong. Stan Hugill's version in his book *Shanties from the Seven Seas* does just that. For the most part, this version comes from Hugill, although several verses are from other sources.

Randy Dandy O
Capstan

Now we are war- ping her out from the docks   Way hey   roll and go Those

pret- ty young girls come wave fare-well in flocks To me rol-lic- kin' ran- dy   dan- dy- o

Now we are warping her out from the docks
Chorus: Way, hey, roll and go
Those pretty young girls come wave farewell in flocks
Chorus: To me rollickin' randy dandy o

It's goodbye to all of the girls of this town
We've left you enough for to buy your silk gowns

It's goodbye to Sally, now goodbye to Sue
And all of you other girls farewell to you

We're sick of the shore and our money's all gone
So we signed on this packet to drive her along

Our anchor's aweigh and the wind's drawing free
Let's get the glad rags on her, head her for sea

Oh breast the bars, bullies, now heave with a will
And soon we'll be drivin' her off down the hill

We're bound away around Cape Horn
Where you'll wish to the Lord that you'd never been born

Around Cape Horn we all must go
Way off 'round Cape Stiff through the cold rain and snow

So heave a pawl, now heave away
Get crackin' now, lads, it's a mighty long way

Yes, heave a pawl, now heave away
Our anchor's on board and our cable's all stored

20

The first line of this song refers to the process of "warping." Warping a sailing ship involved taking a mooring line to a dock piling and then using the capstan to pull the ship forward. Then, another line was placed on a piling farther up, and the process repeated. The ship could be moved in or out of a harbor without a tug boat. Think about all that work, even before any sails were set! Then, look at the words. What do they say about life ashore and life at sea?

   This is a capstan chantey that Stan Hugill learned from his West Indian shipmate Harding, "the Barbadian Barbarian," who said he had used it on a Nova Scotian bark. Hugill says it was "very popular on the old Cape Horners." Some versions use the last verse as a "Grand Chorus," sung after every verse by the whole crew.

Santianno
Capstan

We're sail- ing 'cross the riv- er from Liv- er- pool Heave a-

way San- ti a- nno A- round Cape Horn to 'Fris- co Bay All a-

cross the plains of Mex- i- co So heave her up and a-

way we'll go Heave a- way San- ti a- nno Heave her up and a-

way we'll go All a- cross the plains of Mex- i- co

We're sailing 'cross the river from Liverpool
Chorus: Heave away, Santianno
Around Cape Horn to 'Frisco Bay
Chorus: All across the plains of Mexico

Grand Chorus
So heave her up and away we'll go
Heave away, Santianno
Heave her up and away we'll go
All across the plains of Mexico

We got a bully clipper ship and a bully, bully crew
Heave away, Santianno
A down east Yankee for a captain, too
All across the plains of Mexico

Oh, Santianno was a mighty fine man
Heave away, Santianno
Until he made war with Uncle Sam
All across the plains of Mexico

Oh, General Taylor gained the day
Heave away, Santianno
He made old Santy run away
All across the plains of Mexico

Oh, when I was a young man and in my prime
Heave away, Santianno
I'd court them young gals ten at a time
All across the plains of Mexico

Now I'm old and turning grey
Heave away, Santianno
Them pretty young gals all walk the other way
All across the plains of Mexico

Now when my sailing days are done
Heave away, Santianno
I'll settle down with my Betsy Brown
All across the plains of Mexico

Sung at the capstan, this chantey tells the story of the Mexican general Santa Ana, who fought against the United States in the Mexican War (1846-1848). Some Americans believed that the Pacific Ocean was the natural western boundary of the United States. The Mexican War succeeded in adding large tracts of territory to the United States as the nineteenth-century idea of "manifest destiny" fueled westward expansion. Nonetheless, the war led to the political defeat of the Democratic party, which supported the war. It also set up future problems, culminating in the Civil War (1861-1865). In this version, we hear the truth about the victory of General Zachary Taylor, U.S. Army. This chantey was a favorite of whalers.

Halyard Chanteys

The "engine" of a sailing ship was its sails. On square-rigged ships, the sails hung from wooden cross-pieces called yards. These yards were movable. They would be hauled up to set a sail and lowered back down when the sail was furled (put away). Between canvas and stick, the yard and sail could easily weigh over 1,000 pounds, and on some big ships upwards of 2,500 pounds. By lowering all of this weight closer to the deck when the sail was not in use, the ship became more stable as its center of gravity was lowered.

Setting sail required that the crew first go aloft into the rigging of the ship to loosen the canvas sail. Once back on deck, the crew would take hold of a line called the halyard. Literally, "halyard" is a combination of the two words "haul" and "yard." A halyard chantey helped all of the people on the line pull together. During the verses, the crew would rest, but during the chorus, they would all pull together, like a group playing tug o' war. Usually, the chorus gave the crew two strong beats to pull twice on the halyard. Sometimes, however, the job was heavier, so they would only get one pull per chorus. Other times, the job might be lighter, and the crew could pull three times or even hand-over-hand on regular beats throughout both verse and chorus. The underlined syllables in each song show where the sailors would pull.

Hello Somebody
Halyard

Somebody's knockin' at the garden gate
Chorus: He<u>ll</u>o, somebody, <u>hell</u>o
It's Bully John and his dirty mate
Chorus: He<u>ll</u>o, somebody, <u>hell</u>o

Bully John from Baltimore
I knew him well on the Eastern Shore

Well Bully John is the mate for me
He's a bully on land and a bucko at sea

Oh Bully John I knew him well
But now he's dead and he's roastin' in the fires of . . .

Oh, eight little sailors went up to heaven
Well, one looked back and now there's seven

Around Cape Horn we all must go
Around Cape Horn through the frost and the snow

This African-Caribbean chantey is preserved in William Doerflinger's *Shantymen and Shantyboys*. He attributes it to a chanteyman who went by the name of "Lemon" Curtis. It tells the story of "Bully John," a "bucko mate," and what happened to him. Do you think that you would like to have a "bucko mate" for a boss? A great number of verses from other halyard chanteys also work within the simple construction of "Hello Somebody." This version is a combination of verses found in Doerflinger, Frederick Pease Harlow's *Chanteying Aboard American Ships*, and Hugill's works.

Hieland Laddie
Halyard

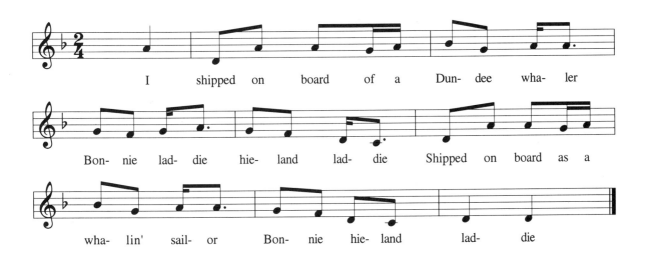

I shipped on board of a Dundee whaler
Chorus: Bonnie laddie, hieland laddie
Shipped on board as a whalin' sailor
Chorus: Bonnie hieland laddie

Sailed far North through the ice and snow
Way far North where the whalefish blow

Greenland is a cold country
Not the place for you and me

Caught some whales and boiled the blubber
Oil and fat choke every scupper

I'll be glad when I get hame [home]
I'll give up this whalin' game

Oh hieland laddie went a-sailin'
Oh hieland laddie went a-whalin'

Only a handful of chanteys mention the theme of whaling within their texts. The town of Dundee, Scotland, had a fleet of whaleships sailing in the nineteenth century. As one might expect, the origins of "Hieland Laddie" are found in an old Scottish march and dance tune. This version of the chantey is in the group of the two-pull halyard type. Other versions of this song, some with four-line choruses, were used as capstan or walk-away chanteys. Most verses are taken from Stan Hugill's book *Shanties from the Seven Seas*; however, verse number two, though born from the flavor of tradition, is in fact contemporary in its origin.

Hieland Laddie (B) This is the more popular version of the song. Instead of mentioning a whaling voyage, its lyrics are a roster of ports that a deepwater sailor might visit and the things that he might do there.

Was you ev- er in Que- bec Bon- nie lad- die hie- land lad- die

Stow- ing tim- ber on the deck Bon- nie hie- land lad- die

Way hey and a- way we'll go Bon- nie lad- die hie- land lad- die

Way hey and a- way we'll go My bon- nie hie- land lad- die

Additional lyrics in this version follow:

> Was you ever in Mobile Bay?
> *Chorus* Bonnie laddie, hieland laddie
> Screwing cotton all the day?
> *Chorus* Bonnie hieland laddie
>
> *Grand Chorus*
> Way, hey, and away we go,
> Way, hey, and away we go
>
> Was you ever in Miramashee?
> Where you tie up to a tree?
>
> Was you ever in Baltimore?
> Dancing on the sanded floor?
>
> Was you ever around Cape Horn?
> Where you'd wish to god you'd never been born?

A Long Time Ago
Halyard

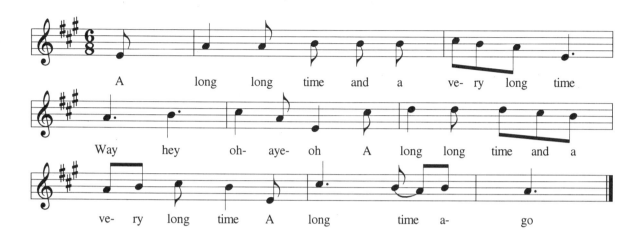

A long, long time and a very long time
Chorus: Way hey oh-aye-oh
A long, long time and a very long time
Chorus: A long time ago

Three ships they lay out there in the bay
Three ships they lay out there in the bay

One of the ships was the old Noah's Ark
Trim-rigged and flashy and covered with bark

The animals came on two by two
Until the old Ark looked just like a zoo

But the bull and the cow, they started a row
Noah jumped up and said, "Way enough now"

The bull put his horn through the side of the Ark
The little brown dog then began to bark

Noah stuck the dog's nose in the hole
Since then all dog's noses have been wet and cold

It's a long, long time and a very long time
A long, long time and a very long time

Some chanteys are whimsical or nonsensical, similar to old wives' tales, folk tales, or tall tales. Finally solving the question of why dogs' noses are wet and cold, "A Long Time Ago" is typical of the humor used by sailors to relieve the tedium of their work. Many chanteys use a familiar theme, in this case Noah's Ark, as their structure. This version is based primarily on the version found in Stan Hugill's *Shanties from the Seven Seas.*

John Cherokee
Halyard

Oh this is the sto-ry of John Cher-o-kee Al-a-bam-a John Cher-o-kee An

In-di-an man from Mir-a-ma-shee Al-a-bam-a John Cher-o-kee

Way hey yah Al-a-bam-a John Cher-o-kee

Oh, this is the story of John Cherokee
Chorus: Alabama, John Cherokee
An Indian man from Miramashee
Chorus: Alabama, John Cherokee
Way, hey, yah!
Chorus: Alabama, John Cherokee

Now, John Cherokee was an Indian man
They made him a slave down in Alabam'

Now they made him a slave on a whaling ship
But again and again he gave 'em the slip

They catched him again and they chained him tight
And they kept him chained up both the day and night

Gave [him] nothin' to eat and nothin' to drink
Until his bones begin to clink

Gave him nothin' to drink and nothin' to eat
'Til he drop dead at the captain's feet

And now his ghost it can be seen
A-sittin' on the main truck wet and green

Before the Civil War, plantation owners sometimes sent their slaves to sea. This might have been done to prevent running away, as punishment, or to bring in money for the slave holder. The slave received no cash payment, but going to sea sometimes meant being treated equally with the rest of the crew. This chantey tells a somewhat strange story that raises questions about Native Americans and slavery. Part of what makes the story strange is that John Cherokee was from Canada, as "Miramashee" is the Miramichi River in New Brunswick. Apparently, whoever made John Cherokee a slave saw no distinction between an African and a Native American. Sources are Stan Hugill's *Shanties From the Seven Seas* and his live performances, and Joanna Colcord's *Roll and Go*.

Lowlands Low
Topgallant halyard

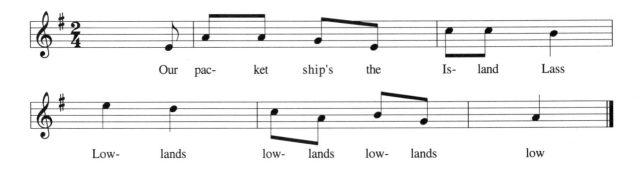

Our packet ship's the *Island Lass*
Chorus: Lowlands, lowlands, lowlands low
There's a sailor howling from the main topmast
Chorus: Lowlands, lowlands, lowlands low

Our old man hails from Barbados
They call his name "Old Hammertoes"

Our first mate's rigged in soldier's clothes
Where he got 'em God alone knows

It's Lowlands, boys, and up she goes
Way up aloft from down below

They fed us bread as hard as brass
And the meat's as salty as Lot's wife's . . . feet

It's Lowlands, boys, now up she goes
Get changed now, boys, to your shore-going clothes

Stan Hugill learned this chantey from his West Indian shipmate Tobago Smith. As in many songs from the Caribbean, notice the lack of similarity between each verse. Stan sang this song at Mystic Seaport's Sea Music Festival with great energy and a driving rhythm. The topgallant sail, or t'gallant, and the royal, are some of the highest sails on a ship. *Three* pulls on the chorus, rather than the usual two, are used for these smaller, lighter squaresails.

Reuben Ranzo
Halyard

Oh poor old Reu- ben Ran- zo Ran- zo boys Ran- zo He

sold his plow and har- row Ran- zo me boys Ran- zo

Oh poor old Reuben Ranzo
Chorus: <u>Ran</u>zo, boys, <u>Ran</u>zo
He sold his plow and harrow
Chorus: <u>Ran</u>zo, me boys, <u>Ran</u>zo

Old Ranzo was no sailor
So they shipped him on board of a whaler

Ranzo was no beauty
He could not do his duty

He's done his hair with oil
But he could not furl a royal

They took him to the gangway
They give him lashes twenty

The skipper ordered thirty
But his daughter begged for mercy

She took him in the cabin
She give him rum and brandy

Aye, she give him wine and water
And a bit more than she oughter [ought to]

She taught him navigation
And she give him education

He married the old man's daughter
He's sailin' on blue water

Now Ranzo he's a skipper
Aboard a Yankee clipper

I wish I was old Ranzo's son
I'd build a ship of a thousand ton

A shining ship of a thousand ton
And I'd give me sailors plenty of rum

But now old Ranzo's dead and gone
No one to sing his funeral song

This chantey is used for hauling up the heavy sails on the *Charles W. Morgan* and *Joseph Conrad*. One of many sources for this song is A.L. Lloyd's album *Sea Shanties*. However, the origins of the name "Reuben Ranzo" are often debated. According to Stan Hugill, Reuben might refer to the term "Rube," American slang for a greenhand, an inexperienced sailor. Ranzo is possibly short for Lorenzo, a name that suggests Portuguese descent. Many Azoreans (Portuguese) became whalemen. In the text Ranzo starts out as a greenhand who knows next to nothing about being a sailor. By the end of the song, he has been taught navigation and improved his status by marrying the captain's daughter. Have you ever known anyone who has had an advantage because of *whom* he knew rather than *what* he knew?

Roll the Old Chariot
Walk-away halyard

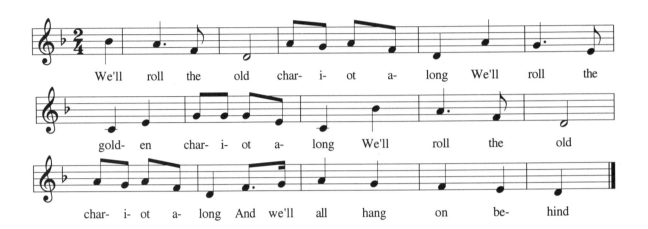

We'll roll the old char- i- ot a- long We'll roll the
gold- en char- i- ot a- long We'll roll the old
char- i- ot a- long And we'll all hang on be- hind

Chorus
We'll roll the old chariot along
We'll roll the golden chariot along
We'll roll the old chariot along
And we'll all hang on behind

Oh a drop of Nelson's blood wouldn't do us any harm
A drop of Nelson's blood wouldn't do us any harm
A drop of Nelson's blood wouldn't do us any harm
And we'll all hang on behind

Oh a plate of Irish stew wouldn't do us any harm
A plate of Irish stew wouldn't do us any harm
A plate of Irish stew wouldn't do us any harm
And we'll all hang on behind

Oh a night on the shore wouldn't do us any harm
A night on the shore wouldn't do us any harm
A night on the shore wouldn't do us any harm
And we'll all hang on behind

"Roll the Old Chariot" is similar in construction to the more famous song "Drunken Sailor." Both of these songs were used to haul up sails. The crew picked up the halyard and marched down the deck until they ran out of room. When they reached the end, they turned around, ran back, picked up the halyard again, and continued marching down the deck. This went on until the sail was raised all the way. A walk-away halyard chantey, also called a stomp-and-go, could only be employed when a square-rigger had a crew large enough to do this type of hauling. This chantey no doubt evolved from a black spiritual.

Shallow Brown
Halyard

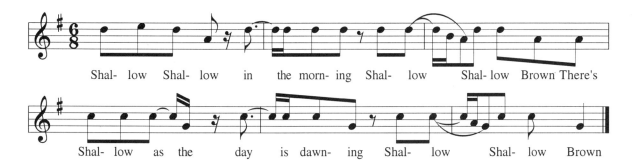

Shal- low Shal- low in the morn- ing Shal- low Shal- low Brown There's

Shal- low as the day is dawn- ing Shal- low Shal- low Brown

Shallow, Shallow in the morning
Chorus: Shallow, Shallow Brown
There's Shallow as the day is dawning
Chorus: Shallow, Shallow Brown

I thought I heard the old man say
Tomorrow is our sailing day

The blackbird sang, the crow said "caw"
Let's get this sail set by half past four

The blackbird said unto the crow
I think it's time we roll and go

We're bound away for Baltimore
To dance upon that sanded floor

We're bound away around Cape Horn
That's where the winds are never warm

My wife and baby they do grieve me
It breaks my heart for me to leave you

Oh, I love you, Julianna
Oh, yes, I love you, Julianna

This lovely and tuneful halyard chantey is of West Indian origin and lends itself well to harmony on the chorus. Several melodies are given in collections. The verses in this version are cobbled together from a variety of sources, including some other songs like "Hilo, Come Down Below" from Stan Hugill for the "bird verses." The melancholy mood of this song works well on a sweltering August day when the crew is tired and hot and nobody wants to hear anything cheerful.

Short Drag Chanteys

Sometimes a job was so difficult that the crew could only pull one time during each chorus. Short drag chanteys were used when two-pull, three-pull, or hand-over-hand chanteys would have been too much work for the crew. Typically, these jobs were adjusting (trimming) sails or pulling the last few times while raising a yard (mastheading). At Mystic Seaport, our most common use of a short drag chantey is raising the whaleboat on the *Charles W. Morgan*. Again, the underlined word in each song is where the crew would pull together.

Boney
Short drag

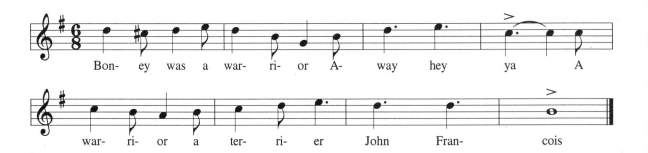

Bon- ey was a war- ri- or A- way hey ya A war- ri- or a ter- ri- er John Fran- cois

Boney was a warrior
Chorus: Away hey <u>ya</u>
A warrior, a terrier
Chorus: John Fran<u>cois</u>

Boney was a Corsican
A rortin' snortin' Corsican

Boney was a general
A randy dandy general

Boney fought the Rooshians
The Austrians and Prooshians

Boney went to Moscow
He lost his army in the snow

Boney went to Elbow
And Boney he come back again

Boney went to Waterloo
And there he got a-overthrew

Boney he was sent away
Away to St. Helena

Away to St. Helena
Aboard the *Billy Ruffian*

Boney broke his heart and died
Away in St. Helena

They put poison in his food
Oh, it didn't do him any good

Boney he is dead and gone
And we will sing his funeral song

Boney was a warrior
A warrior, a terrier

This song was sung by British sailors both to honor and to make fun of their enemy, the French Emperor Napoleon Bonaparte (1769-1821). Napoleon gained his fame through military victories. His armies fought with all of the powers of Europe at one time or another, especially, as the song says, the Russians (Rooshians) and Prussians (Prooshians). In France, he was made "First Consul" (1799), then "Consul for Life" (1802), then finally Emperor (1804). He was also crowned King of Italy in 1805. Fighting with all of those people made Napoleon a lot of enemies. He was banished first to Elba (Elbow) and then to St. Helena, where he died. It has been suggested through evidence recently brought to light that he may have died as a result of arsenic poisoning. In this version, the reference to poison is a variation of the traditional verse.

Dan Dan
Short drag

My name it is Dan Dan *Chorus*: <u>argh</u>
My name it is Dan Dan *Chorus*: <u>argh</u>
Somebody stole my rum *Chorus*: <u>argh</u>
He didn't leave me none *Chorus*: <u>argh</u>
That no good son of a gun *Chorus*: <u>argh</u>

My name it is Dan Dan
A sailor man I am
Somebody took my wife
Somebody took my knife
My name it is Dan Dan

This West Indian chant/chantey probably started out as a shore song. Stan Hugill, in *Shanties from the Seven Seas*, again lists Harding as his primary source. The room to improvise in this song is huge, as almost any article of clothing or gear could be stolen. As a chantey, this is used frequently for hauling up the whaleboat on the *Charles W. Morgan*. Its quick pace keeps things moving nicely along. It is also used frequently in music programs to loosen up groups who are intimidated by singing in front of their friends since "that grunt noise isn't really singing."

Bring 'Em Down
Short drag

In Liv- er- pool I was born Bring 'em down

On a cold Oc- to- ber morn Bring 'em down

Lon- don is me home from home Bring 'em down

When I'm not sail- ing on the foam Bring 'em down

In Liverpool I was born
Chorus: <u>Bring</u> 'em down
On a cold October morn
Chorus: <u>Bring</u> 'em down
London is me home from home
Chorus: <u>Bring</u> 'em down
When I'm not sailing on the foam
Chorus: <u>Bring</u> 'em down

Spend my time in the Black Ball Line
Never a day behind the time
'Round Cape Stiff we all must go
Through the rain, the ice and snow

Up the coast to Vallipo
Northward bound to Callao
Those Callao girls I do adore
They'll dance all night, they'll ask for more

We're in Desolation Bay
Hanging around from day to day
Blow ye wind, now 'way ye blow
Rise up ya bugger, now let us go

We're homeward bound to Liverpool
Spend my money just like a fool
Spend my money on a week on shore
To go to sea and scratch for more

We're Liverpool born and bred
Thick in the arms and thick in the head
Rock and roll me over boys
Let's get this job over boys

A great example of the joining of two distinct styles of chanteying, "Bring 'Em Down" demonstrates the meeting of the Anglo-Irish and African-Caribbean traditions. A fun short drag, the pull comes on the word "bring." This version has a story of sorts, typical of Anglo-Irish chanteys, but its loose structure provides room for improvising, common in American chanteys. Again, A.L. Lloyd's album *Sea Shanties* is the source.

Haul Away, Joe
Short drag

Oh when I was a lit- tle boy or so my mo- ther told me Way haul a- way we'll haul a- way Joe

Oh, when I was a little boy, or so my mother told me,
Chorus: Way, haul away, we'll haul away Joe!
That if I did not kiss the girls my lips would all grow moldy
Chorus: Way, haul away, we'll haul away Joe!

Grand Chorus
So, way, haul away, oh haul and sing together,
Way, haul away, we'll haul away Joe!
So, way, haul away, oh haul for better weather,
Way, haul away, we'll haul away Joe!

Saint Patrick was a gentle man, he came from decent people
Way, haul away, we'll haul away Joe!
In Dublin town he built a church and on it put a steeple
Way, haul away, we'll haul away Joe!

King Louis was the king of France before the revolution
Way, haul away, we'll haul away Joe!
But then he got his head cut off, it spoiled his constitution
Way, haul away, we'll haul away Joe!

Once in my life I married a wife but she was fat and lazy
Way, haul away, we'll haul away Joe!
And then I got a Yankee gal, she nearly drove me crazy
Way, haul away, we'll haul away Joe!

Short drag chanteys of this type were very handy to synchronize a few strong, hard pulls. "Haul Away, Joe" was often used to trim sails when a few short, quick tugs were needed to fight both wind pressure and the weight of the canvas and yards. The long phrase ending with the pull on "Joe!" would have been far less popular when used on a longer job like raising a boat. Stan Hugill believes that this chantey could also be used as a two-pull halyard because of the great number of verses. The rhyming couplets reveal the sailor's wry sense of humor.

Haul On the Bowline
Short drag

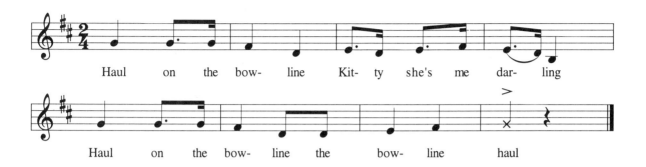

Haul on the bowline
Kitty she's me darling
Chorus: Haul on the bowline, the bowline <u>haul</u>

Haul on the bowline
Kitty she's in Liverpool

Haul on the bowline
Kitty she's a lovely girl

Haul on the bowline
I took my Kitty for a walk

Haul on the bowline
You cannot tie a bowline

A pint of rum, a glass of beer
A sailor likes his pint of rum

Stan Hugill suggests that this chantey is fairly ancient. The bowline, as a part of a vessel's running rig, became insignificant early in the development of deepwater sailing vessels. This is used as a standard short drag at Mystic Seaport, although Hugill lists a capstan version. Again, this type of song is open to improvisation. Some other verses contain the following lines after "Haul on the bowline": "so early in the morning," "the bully, bully bowline," "the long-tailed bowline," "oh haul away together."

Windlass and Pumping Chanteys

A windlass is another machine used to raise the anchor. It is worked by pumping handles up and down, much like the railroad hand-cars commonly seen in cartoons and old Western movies. As the handles, or brakes, are pumped up and down, the barrel of the windlass rotates and brings in whatever is wrapped around it, usually the anchor chain. Like capstan work, windlass work is often long, hard, and repetitive.

Similar to a windlass are the pumps on board ships. The songs used at one machine are often used at the other. Ships are fitted out with pumps so that during a voyage, the lowest part of the ship, the bilge, can be emptied of water. All wooden ships leak, but so long as the leak is not faster than the crew can pump, everything is all right. Pumps come in several different styles, but for the most part are operated with the same motions as a windlass. Perhaps the one exception to this is the "Downton" pump. This type of pump has a wheel to turn and, attached to the wheel, a rope to pull. Therefore, a sailor can both heave (push) on the wheel and haul (pull) on the rope. It is rare that these two words are combined in the same song, but several versions of "Cape Cod Girls" have a chorus of "heave away, haul away" for this specific use. "Cape Cod Girls" is a great example of just how many variations of the same song can exist.

Cape Cod Girls
Windlass/pumps

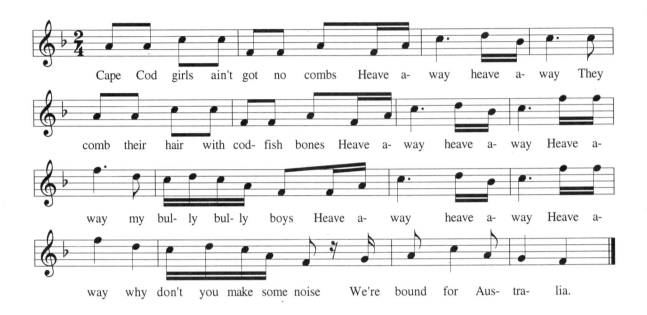

Cape Cod girls ain't got no combs Heave a- way heave a- way They comb their hair with cod- fish bones Heave a- way heave a- way Heave a- way my bul- ly bul- ly boys Heave a- way heave a- way Heave a- way why don't you make some noise We're bound for Aus- tra- lia.

Cape Cod girls ain't got no combs
Chorus: Heave away, heave away
They comb their hair with codfish bones
Chorus: Heave away, heave away

Grand Chorus
Heave away, my bully, bully boys
Heave away, heave away
Heave away, why don't you make some noise?
We're bound for Australia

Cape Cod boys ain't got no sleds
Heave away, heave away
They slide down hills on codfish heads
Heave away, heave away

Cape Cod doctors got no pills
Heave away, heave away
They feed their patients codfish gills
Heave away, heave away

Cape Cod cats ain't got no tails
Heave away, heave away
They all blew off in them Cape Cod gales
Heave away, heave away

Cape Cod moms don't bake no pies
Heave away, heave away
They feed their children codfish eyes
Heave away, heave away

This chantey is used at the windlass on the *L.A. Dunton*. Almost any part of a codfish might find its way into this chantey, making it a great song to improvise when needed. Perhaps you can come up with some verses of your own! There are many different versions of "Cape Cod Girls," some with different choruses, some with different rhythms, and some with different melodies. We have presented several of these variations here.

Cape Cod Girls (B) This is considered to be the most common way to sing this song. Note the two different words in the chorus—heave away, haul away. This construction shows the flexibility of the song for both windlass and pumping work.

Cape Cod girls ain't got no combs Heave a- way haul a- way They
comb their hair with cod- fish bones And we're bound for Aus- tra- lia
Heave a- way my bul- ly bul- ly boys Heave- a- way haul a- way
Heave 'er up and won't you make some noise And we're bound for Aus- tra- lia

Cape Cod Girls (C) This is Stan Hugill's version, from his book *Shanties from the Seven Seas*. It demonstrates the influence that an individual singer can have on a piece. It is very similar to version B, but contains examples of Stan's own unique vocal inflections.

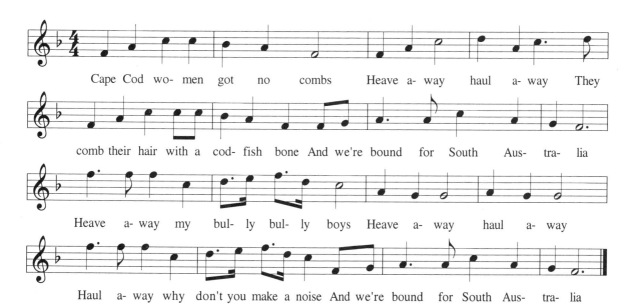

Cape Cod wo- men got no combs Heave a- way haul a- way They
comb their hair with a cod- fish bone And we're bound for South Aus- tra- lia
Heave a- way my bul- ly bul- ly boys Heave a- way haul a- way
Haul a- way why don't you make a noise And we're bound for South Aus- tra- lia

Cape Cod Girls (D) This version appears to be very popular with contemporary singers in the greater New York City area.

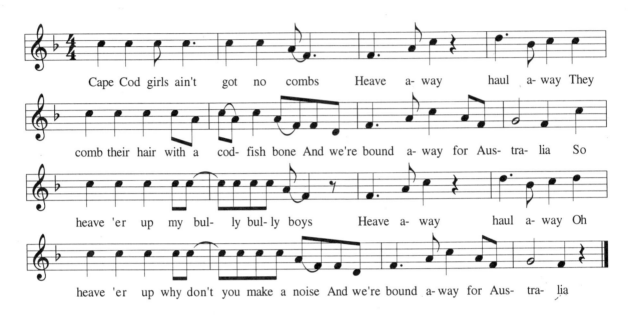

Cape Cod girls ain't got no combs Heave a- way haul a- way They
comb their hair with a cod- fish bone And we're bound a- way for Aus- tra- lia So
heave 'er up my bul- ly bul- ly boys Heave a- way haul a- way Oh
heave 'er up why don't you make a noise And we're bound a- way for Aus- tra- lia

Cape Cod Girls (E) With a slightly different chorus, this version may be the result of singers taking the words from one song and applying them to the tune of another. Overall, the many different ways to sing this single song show the great variation possible in an oral tradition.

Cape Cod girls ain't got no combs Heave a- way haul a- way They
comb their hair with a cod- fish bone And we're bound for South Aus- tra- lia
Haul a- way you roll- ing king Heave a- way haul a- way
All the way you'll hear me sing And we're bound for South Aus- tra- lia

49

Paddy Works on the Railway
Windlass/pumps

In eigh- teen hun- dred and six- ty one I put my cord-u- roy brit- ches on The A- mer-i- can rail- road just be- gun A- work- ing on the rail- way Fid- dle me o- ree- o- ree- ay Fid- dle me o- ree- o- ree- ay Fid- dle me o- ree- o- ree- ay Work- ing on the rail- way

In eighteen hundred and sixty-one
I put my corduroy britches on
The American railroad just begun
A-working on the railway

Chorus
Fiddle me or-ree-or-ree-ay
Fiddle me or-ree-or-ree-ay
Fiddle me or-ree-or-ree-ay
Working on the railway

In eighteen hundred and sixty-two
I'm looking around for something to do
Looking around for something to do
But work upon the railway

In eighteen hundred and sixty-three
I thought that I should go to sea
But the 'Merican railroad hired me
I'm working on the railway

In eighteen hundred and sixty-four
I found my back was mighty sore
Found my back was mighty sore
From working on the railway

In eighteen hundred and sixty-five
I found myself more dead than alive
Found myself more dead than alive
From working on the railway

In eighteen hundred and sixty-six
Found myself in a whale of a fix
Stepped in a pile of dynamite sticks
Working on the railway

In eighteen hundred and sixty-seven
My children now they numbered eleven
Of boys I'd four, girls I'd seven
Working on the railway

In eighteen hundred and sixty-eight
I finally got rich but far too late
I was picking pearls at the Pearly Gates
Working on the railway

Many people learned this chantey in grade school. Mystic Seaport chanteyman Marc Bernier learned this version from his fourth-grade teacher, Pete Lirot. Stan Hugill is almost certain that this chantey started out as a land song and then went to sea. According to Stan, this is the land version. It was very popular at the windlass, pumps, and capstan. This chantey is used quite a bit in music programs to demonstrate land and sea traditions coming together, as well as the joining of Anglo-Irish and African-Caribbean traditions. The opportunity exists to have students add verses chronologically, as a chanteyman might have done.

Paddy Works on the Railway (B) This is the version that Stan Hugill printed in *Shanties from the Seven Seas*. He considers this to be the sea-going adaptation of a land-based song.

Roll the Woodpile Down
Windlass/pumps

Way down South where the cocks do crow Way down in Flor- i- da Them

girls they dance to the old ban- jo And we'll roll the wood- pile down

Roll- in' (Roll- in') Roll- in' (Roll- in') Roll- in' the whole world 'round That

brown gal of mine on the Geor- gia line And we'll roll the wood-pile down.

Way down South where the cocks do crow
Chorus: Way down, in Florida
Them girls they dance to the old banjo
Chorus: And we'll roll the woodpile down

Grand Chorus
Rollin' (*Repeat*: Rollin')
Rollin' (*Repeat*: Rollin')
Rollin' the whole world 'round
That brown gal of mine on the Georgia line
And we'll roll the woodpile down

Oh, rouse and bust her is the cry
Way down in Florida
A sailor's wage is never high
And we'll roll the woodpile down

When I was a young man in me prime
Way down in Florida
I chased them pretty girls three at a time
And we'll roll the woodpile down

But now I'm old and turning grey
Way down in Florida
Them pretty young girls they all look away
And we'll roll the woodpile down

Oh, Curly goes on the old ran-tan
Way down in Florida
Curly's just a Downeast man
And we'll roll the woodpile down

We'll heave her high and we'll heave her low
Way down in Florida
We'll heave her up and away we'll go
And we'll roll the woodpile down

Oh, one more heave and that will do
Way down in Florida
And we're the bullies for to kick her through
And we'll roll the woodpile down

This windlass and pumping chantey was sung by black chanteymen and originated in the southern United States. Where "Paddy Lay Back" tells a story from start to finish, "Roll the Woodpile Down" tells stories within individual verses. Verses can be sung in any order and a story line is not disturbed. This is, again, often characteristic of chanteys from the African-Caribbean tradition. The crew would respond on the chorus lines within each verse, then all join together for the grand chorus with its call and response to "Rollin'." When the job of pumping the ship was complete, the cry of "suck-o," meaning that the pump was drawing only air, would be yelled.

Strike the Bell
Windlass/pumps

Aft on the poop deck wal- king all a- bout

There's the sec- ond mate so stead- y and so stout

What he's a- thin- king he knows not him- self [but] We're

wish- ing he would hur- ry up and strike strike the bell

Strike the bell sec- ond mate let us go be- low

Look you well to wind- ward you can see it's going to blow

Look at the glass you see that it has fell And we

wish that you would hur- ry up and strike strike the bell

Aft on the poop deck, walking all about
There's the second mate so steady and so stout
What he's a-thinking, he knows not himself [but]
We're wishing he would hurry up and strike, strike the bell!

Chorus:
Strike the bell, second mate, let us go below
Look you well to windward, you can see it's going to blow
Look at the glass, you can see that it has fell
And we wish that you would hurry up and strike, strike the bell

Now, down on the main deck and working at the pumps
There's the larboard watch, just longing for their bunks
Looking to the windward, they see a great swell
And they're wishing that the second mate would strike, strike the bell

Oh, aft at the wheel, poor Anderson stands
Clutching at the spokes with his cold and mittened hands
Looking at the compass head, the course is sure and well
And he's wishing that the second mate would strike, strike the bell

Well, forward on the fo'c's'le head and keeping sharp lookout
There's Johnny standing, ready for to shout
The lights are burning bright, sir, everything is well
We're wishing that the second mate would strike, strike the bell

Oh aft on the quarterdeck, our gallant captain stands
Looking at the sea with a spyglass in his hand
What he's a-thinking, we all know very well
He's thinking more of shortening sail than—strike the bell!

"Strike the Bell" is used at the windlass on the *L.A. Dunton* and the *Charles W. Morgan*. It could also be used at the pumps. The lyrics talk about shipboard life and work. At the beginning of a voyage, the crew was divided up into two groups—the port (here called "larboard") watch and the starboard watch. Each worked for four hours, then had four hours off while the other group worked. It was impossible to get more than three-and-a-half hours of sleep at any one time! If the ship needed attention, the officers would call "All hands on deck!" This meant that the sailors had to work even if it was their turn to have time off. Sometimes they would miss what little time that they had for sleep and were up even longer. The characters in this song are asking the second mate to strike the bell and send them below. They want to warm up a little before the captain calls "all hands" to put away the sails.

1. The Procession.　　2. The Auction.　　3. Last of the Dead Horse.

THE DEAD HORSE FESTIVAL.

Ceremonial Chanteys and Fo'c's'le Songs

The demands of shipboard work left sailors little leisure time, but music played an important role here as well. Fo'c's'le songs were not work songs; they were songs sung by sailors during their limited time off. They often told stories of heroes and villains, famous battles, romances, or a longing for home. Sailors sang many songs extolling the joys of shore life compared to the dangers and drudgery of shipboard life. Once on shore, however, there were other dangers.

Sailors were one of the few groups of workers to be paid in hard currency. They were paid in gold at the end of a voyage. Sending sailors on to the shore with all of that money in their pockets was like sending a "kid into a candy store" with a year's worth of allowance. Even worse, there were people on the shore who wanted to take the sailor's hard-earned money any way that they could. They might overcharge a sailor for clothing, food, and beverage or they might steal his money outright. Between the temptations of the shore and the "landsharks" preying on them, a sailor might spend a year's worth of salary in a few days.

A sailor then had little choice but to go back to sea. When he signed on again, the shipping company traditionally gave the sailor one month's pay in advance. The idea was that the sailor would buy all of the gear that he needed—sea boots, a knife, a cup and plate, foul weather gear—with the advance money. Sometimes, a sailor was shipped on board by an unscrupulous shipping agent called a "crimp." The crimp took the sailor's advance money from the company and recruited sailors any way possible. "Shanghaiing," being kidnapped and sent out to sea, was common. One way or another, a sailor had lost his first month's pay.

"Poor Old Horse," the Dead Horse chantey, was traditionally sung at the end of the first month at sea. The image of a horse probably came from horse-trading. Once a deal was sealed with a handshake, there was no trading back. Payment still had to be made even if the horse immediately dropped dead. Paying for something that could no longer be used was like working for money that had already been spent. To celebrate the end of the sailors' debt to the ship, a "dead horse"—fashioned from shipboard scrap, old canvas, worn rope, and the like—was dragged about the deck, hoisted aloft, and tossed into the ocean. Sailors had very little opportunity for fun on board ship. The dead horse ceremony was one of the few times that the sailors could blow off steam. Their next chance was when the ship crossed the Equator. A "Crossing the Line" ceremony, where the greenhands would meet King Neptune and enter his brotherhood, was next. This type of "skylarking"—taking time off to fool around and have fun— helped to relieve the monotony of a long deep-sea voyage. "Poor Old Horse" could also be used as a halyard chantey.

Rolling Down To Old Maui
Whaling ballad

'Tis a rough tough life of toil and strife we whale- men un- der

go And we don't give a damn [when] the gales are done how hard the winds do

blow Aye we're home- ward bound it's a damn fine sound on a

good ship taut and free And we don't give a damn [when] we

drink our rum with the girls of old Ma- ui Roll- ing down to old Ma-

ui me boys Roll- ing down to old Ma- ui We're

home- ward bound from the Arc- tic ground Roll- ing down to old Ma- ui

'Tis a rough, tough life of toil and strife we whalemen undergo
And we don't give a damn, [when] the gales are done how hard the winds do blow
Aye, we're homeward bound, it's a damn fine sound, on a good ship taut and free
And we don't give a damn, [when] we drink our rum with the girls of old Maui

Chorus
Rolling down to old Maui, me boys
Rolling down to old Maui
We're homeward bound from the Arctic grounds
Rolling down to old Maui

And now we sail with a northerly gale through the ice and sleet and rain
And them coconut fronds in them tropic lands, oh we soon shall see again
Six hellish months have passed away on the cold Kamchatka Sea
And now we're bound from the Arctic grounds rolling down to old Maui

And we'll heave the lead where old Diamond Head looms up on old Oahu
Our masts and yards are sheathed in ice and the decks are hid from view
Oh, the horrid ice of them sea-cut tiles, that deck, the Arctic Sea
Are miles behind in the frozen wind as we steered for old Maui

And now we sail with a favorable gale towards our island home
Oh, our main yard sprung, all whaling done, and we ain't got far to roam
And the stunsail booms they are carried away, what care we for that sound
A living gale is after us, thank God we're homeward bound

How soft the breeze on the tropic seas now the ice is far astern
And those native maids in their island glades are awaiting our return
And their big black eyes even now look out, hoping some fine day to see
Our baggy sails running 'fore the gales, rolling down to old Maui

And now we're anchored in the bay with the Kanaka all around
With chants and sweet alo-ahoys [alohas] they greet us homeward bound
And now ashore we will have great fun and we'll paint them beaches red
Awaking in the arms of an island maid with a big fat aching head

This grand whaling ballad is about the bowhead whalers of the Western Arctic. Lahaina, on the island of Maui, Hawaii, was the major port for whaling in the Pacific in the mid-1800s. "Kanaka," in the last verse, is a slang term for the native Hawaiians who used to do the hard work in the sugar cane fields. This was the signature song for legendary chanteyman, artist, and author Stan Hugill (1906-1992). "Rolling Down to Old Maui" is a perfect example of a fo'c's'le song, the only one in this collection. There is a large store of these songs. Please refer to the bibliography for more.

Maui (re: A. L. Lloyd) Lloyd's version of Maui is recorded on his album *Leviathan*.

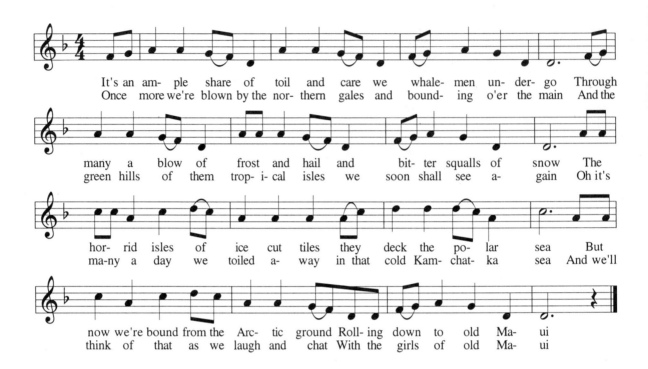

It's an am- ple share of toil and care we whale- men un- der- go Through
Once more we're blown by the nor- thern gales and bound- ing o'er the main And the

many a blow of frost and hail and bit- ter squalls of snow The
green hills of them trop- i- cal isles we soon shall see a- gain Oh it's

hor- rid isles of ice cut tiles they deck the po- lar sea But
ma-ny a day we toiled a- way in that cold Kam- chat- ka sea And we'll

now we're bound from the Arc- tic ground Roll- ing down to old Ma- ui
think of that as we laugh and chat With the girls of old Ma- ui

60

The Dead Horse Chantey
Poor Old Horse
Ceremonial halyard

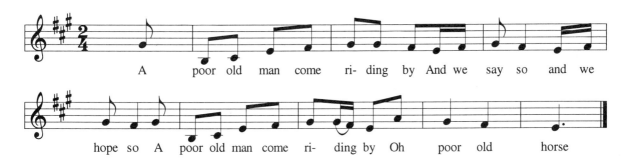

A poor old man come riding by And we say so and we
hope so A poor old man come ri-ding by Oh poor old horse

A poor old man come riding by
Chorus: And we <u>say</u> so, and we <u>hope</u> so
A poor old man come riding by
Chorus: Oh, <u>poor</u> old <u>horse</u>

Says I, "Old man, your horse will die"
Says I, "Old man, your horse will die"

And if he dies we'll tan his skin
And if he don't we'll ride him again

For one long month I rode him hard
For one long month we all rode him hard

But now your month is up, old Turk
Get up, you swine, and look for work

Get up you swine and look for graft
While we lays on and drags ye aft

He's as dead as a nail in the lamp-room door
And he won't come worrying us no more

We'll use the hair of his tail to sew our sails
And the iron of his shoe to make deck nails

We'll hoist him up to the fore yard-arm
Where he won't do sailors any harm

We'll drop him down with a long, long roll
Where the sharks will have his body and the
    devil take his soul

Poor Old Horse (B) This is considered to be the standard version, that is, the variant with which most people are familiar. As is the case with many of these songs, different singers bring their own unique style and vocal timbre to each piece.

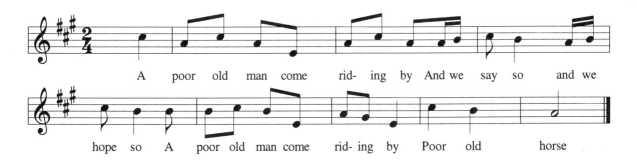

A poor old man come rid-ing by And we say so and we
hope so A poor old man come rid-ing by Poor old horse

This work will provide a platform for a more thorough examination of the wealth of sea music available. There are many fine performers of this style, and contemporary recordings are too numerous to list. Every year, on the second weekend in June, Mystic Seaport hosts a sea music festival. Our festival is the largest of its kind in North America. For more information, please visit us online at www.mysticseaport.org or call our switchboard at (860) 572-0711. Below are both the sources used in this book and some suggestions. Not all are readily available; obtaining some of them will require searching. This, however, is half the fun of keeping traditional music alive.

Bibliography and Suggested Reading

Colcord, Joanna. *Roll and Go*. Indianapolis: The Bobbs-Merrill Co., 1924.
Colcord, Joanna. *Songs of American Sailormen*. New York: Norton, 1938.
Joanna Colcord sailed on board square-riggers as a child. Her father was a captain. *Songs of American Sailormen* is an expanded version of *Roll and Go*. Both are out of print.

Dana, Richard Henry, Jr. *Two Years Before the Mast*. New York: Random House, 1936.
Dana's narrative remains one of the finest accounts of nineteenth-century life at sea. It has been reprinted countless times since its first appearance in 1840.

Doerflinger, William Main. *Shantymen and Shantyboys*. New York: Macmillan, 1951.
Doerflinger's collection is perhaps the most scholarly. Some of his versions are quite unique. Out of print.

Harlow, Frederick Pease. *Chanteying Aboard American Ships*. Barre, MA: Barre Gazette, 1962.
Harlow, Frederick Pease. *The Making of a Sailor*. Salem, MA: Marine Research Society, 1928.
Harlow is the best nineteenth-century source for sea music. His narrative, *The Making of a Sailor*, is considered by some to be the most readable of all similar works. It is mostly prose, but contains a number of chanteys. *Chanteying Aboard American Ships* is all music. It is out of print, but *The Making of a Sailor* has been republished by Dover Books.

Hugill, Stan. *Shanties from the Seven Seas*. London: Routledge & Kegan Paul Ltd., 1961.
      Stan Hugill is the primary twentieth-century source and collector of sea music. He has written many books about sea music, but *Shanties From the Seven Seas* is considered the quintessential work on the subject. It also contains an exhaustive bibliography. This book has been republished by Mystic Seaport.

Huntington, Gale. *Songs the Whalemen Sang*. Barre, MA: Barre Publishers, 1964.
      Huntington's book is another good scholarly source. Out of print.

Lloyd, A. L. *Leviathan*. (Album). London: Topic #12T174, 1967.
Lloyd, A. L. *Sea Shanties*. (Album). London: Topic #12TS234, 1974.
      A. L. Lloyd's albums contain a wealth of both music and information about the songs recorded. Out of print.

Lomax, John, and Alan. *American Ballads and Folk Songs*. New York: Macmillan, 1934.
Lomax, Alan. *The Folk Songs of North America*. Garden City: Doubleday, 1960.
      Both of these books, by a father-and-son team, contain an enormous amount of traditional material. Most of it is land-based, but each has a section on sea music. Out of print, but widely available used.

Palmer, Roy. *Oxford Book of Sea Songs*. Oxford: Oxford University Press, 1986.
      A good collection overall.

Shay, Frank. *American Sea Songs and Chanteys*. New York: Norton, 1948.
Shay, Frank. *A Sailor's Treasury*. New York: Norton, 1951.
      Shay wrote numerous books on the sea, containing both songs and lore. *American Sea Songs and Chanteys* is out of print, but some copies of *A Sailor's Treasury* are still available new.

Glossary

Azores/Azoreans: Three island groups west of and comprising three administrative districts of Portugal (Standard, p. 103). People from the Azores are called Azoreans and were often recruited to serve as whalemen on board whaleships.

'Badian: A shortening of the word "Barbadian," meaning a native of Barbados in the Caribbean.

Bowline: A line or tackle for trimming the foresail of a square-rigger (Rogers, p. 22).

Bramleymoor Dock: A dock in Liverpool, England.

Bucko: A bully (Standard, p. 177). A bucko at sea was usually an officer who drove the men hard.

Bullies: A bully is generally defined as a swaggering, quarrelsome, usually cowardly person who terrorizes weaker people (Standard, p. 180). In chanteys, however, the term "bullies" sometimes can refer to fellow sailors.

Callao: A port city in western Peru, near Lima (Standard, p. 194).

Cape Stiff: Usual sailor name for Cape Horn (Hugill, p. 412).

Corsica/Corsican: An island in the Mediterranean on which Napoleon Bonaparte was born in 1769. The "Corsican" referred to in the song is Napoleon Bonaparte (1769-1821).

Crapoes: Slang word for Frenchmen. French sailors were called Jean Crapaud (John "Toad" or "Frog"), just as English sailors were called John Bull.

Crimp: One who procures the impressment of sailors, soldiers, etc., by decoying or entrapping them (Standard, p. 318).

Desolation Bay: A bay on Desolation Island (also called Kerguelen Island) in the South Indian Ocean.

Downeast: The prevailing winds from New York toward the Gulf of Maine and Nova Scotia blow from west to east. Ships had a downwind sail in that direction, hence "downeast." Going in the other direction, one actually sailed *up* to New York from Maine! In "Roll the Woodpile Down," the "Downeast" man is from Maine.

Dundee, Scotland: A burgh in eastern Scotland, a port on the Firth of Tay (Standard, p. 410); Dundee was a major Scottish whaling port.

Fo'c's'le: Abbreviation of "Forecastle." Now simply the foredeck of a ship or boat, this term formerly meant a raised platform at the bow, often armored, for archers and, later, musketeers. In the 17th to 20th centuries, in many ships it was the location, ergo the name, of the crew's quarters (Rogers, p. 73).

Hilo: A port city in western Peru, not to be confused with Hilo, Hawaii.

Landsharks: Merchants on shore eager to take advantage of sailors on leave and to get as much of the sailors' pay as possible.

Limejuice/Limey: (See "Ebenezer" and Paddy Lay Back"—both words are used) Our nickname, in sailing-ship days and now, for a British ship and her people. Limes and limejuice had been discovered to be a preventative for a common shipboard disease, scurvy; they became a required ration, first in British ships, for this purpose (Rogers, p. 106).

Manifest Destiny: A nineteenth-century concept or philosophy that the United States should expand westward to the Pacific Ocean: it was not only the right but the necessity of Americans to fulfill this destiny.

Mollyhawks: Albatrosses, which are large, web-footed sea birds, with long, narrow wings and hooked beaks (Standard, p. 33, for definition of "albatross").

Nelson: Viscount Horatio Nelson (1758-1805), English admiral, killed at the Battle of Trafalgar (Standard, p. 906). Nelson is considered by many to be Britain's greatest naval officer; he was beloved by seamen.

Pigeonholes: Small compartments, as in a desk: on a capstan, the pigeonholes were small compartments into which were inserted wooden bars to be pushed. The term comes from holes for pigeons to nest in, especially in a compartmented pigeon house (Standard, p. 1023, for latter definition).

Ran-Tan: A sailor's money-spending spree on shore.

Shanghaied: Enforced "volunteering" to raise a crew. The story is too long for this book, but the term originated on San Francisco's notorious Barbary Coast, where men were so recruited to man ships usually sailing in the China trade (Rogers, p. 157).

Skylarking: Now hardly a sea term, although it once was. It meant to romp in the rigging of a sailing ship, such as sliding down the crossjack stay. Lark in this sense comes from the Anglo-Saxon word *lac*, to play (Rogers, p. 162).

Squaresail: Rectangular sails set from yards which pivot about their middle (DeKerchove, p. 771). These sails were called square not because of their shape, but rather because they were set perpendicular, or square, to the hull of a vessel.

Vallipo: A sailor word for Valparaiso (Hugill, p. 417).

Valparaiso: A port city in central Chile (Standard, p. 1480).

Sources Used:

DeKerchove, Rene. *International Maritime Dictionary*, second edition. New York: Van Nostrand Reinhold Company, 1961.

Hugill, Stan. "Glossary." *Shanties from the Seven Seas*. London: Routledge & Kegan Paul, Ltd., 1961.

Rogers, John G. *Origins of Sea Terms*. Mystic, CT: Mystic Seaport Museum, 1985.

"The Standard College Dictionary" in *The Reader's Digest Great Encyclopedic Dictionary*, third edition. Pleasantville, NY: The Reader's Digest Association, 1969.

Acknowledgements

This project would never have come to fruition without involvement from the rest of the Mystic Seaport chantey staff: Marc Bernier, Craig Edwards, Geoff Kaufman, David Littlefield, Don Sineti, Rick Spencer, and Carl Thornton.

Thanks go to Bill Hart, who helped Marc transcribe the music; Mary K Bercaw Edwards, patient proofreader; Maria Christenson, data entry; and Lynn Barker, Marifrances Trivelli, and Jen Stich for technical support. Special thanks go to Geoff Kaufman and Rob Richter, who kept things rolling along. Thank you all. — GG.